THIS IS ME! ACROSTICS

Treasured Gems

Edited By Byron Tobolik

First published in Great Britain in 2023 by:

Young Writers
Remus House
Coltsfoot Drive
Peterborough
PE2 9BF
Telephone: 01733 890066
Website: www.youngwriters.co.uk

All Rights Reserved
Book Design by Ashley Janson
© Copyright Contributors 2023
Softback ISBN 978-1-83565-028-8

Printed and bound in the UK by BookPrintingUK
Website: www.bookprintinguk.com
YB0572E

Foreword

Welcome Reader,

For Young Writers' latest competition *This Is Me Acrostics*, we asked primary school pupils to look inside themselves, to think about what makes them unique, and then write an acrostic poem about it! They rose to the challenge magnificently and the result is this fantastic collection of poems, celebrating them and the things that are important to them.

Here at Young Writers our aim is to encourage creativity in children and to inspire a love of the written word, so it's great to get such an amazing response, with some absolutely fantastic poems. It's important for children to focus on and celebrate themselves and this competition allowed them to write freely and honestly, celebrating what makes them great, expressing their hopes and fears, or simply writing about their favourite things. *This Is Me Acrostics* gave them the power of words.

I'd like to congratulate all the young poets in this anthology, I hope this inspires them to continue with their creative writing.

Contents

Cookridge Primary School, Leeds

Zoe Fry (6)	1
Saheli Katugampola (6)	2
Joud Suleiman (6)	3
Harry Lee (6)	4
Nikita McMillan (7)	5
Emmeline (6)	6
Rosalie Haworth (6)	7
Olivia Coetzee (7)	8
Caleb Hughes-Powell (7)	9
Charlie Halliday (6)	10
Rory Burgener (6)	11
Kyra Filipe (7)	12
George (6)	13
Elaine Starkie (6)	14
Jacob Cable-Watson (6)	15
Summer Lewis (6)	16
Franklin Shirley (6)	17
Oscar Fraser (6)	18
Charlie Page (6)	19
Esther Pierce (5)	20
Emily McKirgan (5)	21
Arin Konal (5)	22
Hudson Brookes (5)	23
Martha Haigh (5)	24
Iris Pottage-Dixon (5)	25
Scarlett Hufton-Alford (5)	26
Samuel Wilkinson (5)	27
Jack Gilder (5)	28
George Haigh (5)	29
Rawa Aziz (5)	30
George M (5)	31
Seth Dixon (5)	32
Grace Wardle (5)	33
Dakota Wilson (6)	34
Sofia Kadiri (5)	35

Craigentinny Primary School, Edinburgh

Chaz Alain Villar (6)	36
Archer Brown (7)	37
Fajr (6)	38
Gabi (7)	39
Yousif Abdelmalik (7)	40
Lucia Salvador Neilson (6)	41
Ella Oni (6)	42
George Clayton (7)	43
Emily Wilson (7)	44
Louie Coleman (7)	45
Emma Gray (7)	46
Amirah Ali (7)	47
Gurjot Kaur (7)	48
Aisha Bayo (7)	49
Maahi (6)	50
Mila Pele (6)	51
Theo Waterson (7)	52
Antos (7)	53
Mia Lawrie (6)	54
Adil Abedin (7)	55
Reece Munro (7)	56
Lily Hamilton (7)	57

Lambton Primary School, Lambton Village

Esmé Hunter (6)	58
Reeva Gallagher (6)	59
Amber Malaugh (6)	60
Ethan Coult (7)	61
Isla Rees (6)	62

Rosie-Ann Richardson (7)	63
Chukwukamso Onyeri (6)	64
Connor Latimer (7)	65
Dylan Kooner (6)	66
Rory Galer (6)	67
Harper Steel (6)	68
Reenay Gallagher (6)	69
Charlie Dawson (6)	70
Saskia Espino-Byrne (6)	71
Peter Wilson (6)	72
Riley Latimer (7)	73

Seaton School, Aberdeen

Melody Essienkan (6)	74
Georgia Singer (6)	75
Moses Souza (7)	76
Damon Knox (7)	77
Alise Kailovica (7)	78
Halin Sattar (7)	79
Willow Dow (7)	80
Axel Olise (7)	81
Rabia Al Masri (7)	82
Nasifa Akter (7)	83
Nela Melnicukova (6)	84
Zach Dick (7)	85

St Patrick's Primary School, Eskra

Ethan Power (6)	86
Orlágh McRory (7)	87
Páidí Shiels (6)	88
Shay Quinn (6)	89
Dara Gortland (6)	90
Conleth McGinley (6)	91
Maya McCaffrey (7)	92
Cillian Kelly (6)	93
Oliver McAnespy (7)	94
Amy Rose McGirr (6)	95
Lorcan McGarvey (6)	96
James McGirr (6)	97
Conor McGinley (6)	98
Amber Lucas (6)	99
Senan McGarvey (6)	100

Claire McMaugh (7)	101

The John Wallis C of E Academy, Kingsnorth

Tallulah Tandy (5)	102
Adelynn Waters (6)	103
Lilly-Rose Harris (5)	104
Lacey-Lou Waller (5)	105
Uwakmfon Monday (6)	106
Yubaraj Gurung (5)	107
Olivia Omoniyi (5)	108
Jackson Longstaff (5)	109
Devian Gurung (6)	110
Octavia Brown (5)	111
Dana-Rose Cooper (5)	112
Archie Gibbs (5)	113
Elaiya C (5)	114
Aishna Pun Phagami (6)	115
Ronnie Burgess (6)	116
Bradley Rees (6)	117
Hunter Harris (5)	118
Ethan McDougall (5)	119
Alyssia Marsh (5)	120
Rielle Watson (5)	121
Olivia Suwala-Suwalski (6)	122
Harley Stubbs (6)	123
Jakub Jasinski (5)	124
Garima Gurung (5)	125
Holly Yarnell (5)	126
Sophia Marchant (6)	127
Pasang Gurung (6)	128
Thomas Butt (5)	129
Lacey Fuller (5)	130
Mason Dray (6)	131
Archer Harris (5)	132
Lily Pietrzak (5)	133
Denis Parker (5)	134
Poppy Warren (6)	135
Riha Ferdousi (6)	136
Kase Williams (5)	137
Ayla Karaoglan (5)	138
Jay Gardiner (5)	139
Dan Paladi (5)	140

Hope Barrett (5)	141
Leon Omoniyi (5)	142
Noah Pyke (5)	143
Zakariya Khosravi (5)	144

The Acrostics

All About Me

A rts and crafts is my favourite thing to do.
L earning English is fun.
L unch is my favourite meal of the day.

A holiday is my favourite part of the summer holidays.
B aths are my favourite part of bedtime.
O utside I like playing on my swing.
U p in the sky, I like watching birds.
T abitha is one of my favourite friends.

M y mummy and daddy are people I love.
E mme is my friend.

Zoe Fry (6)
Cookridge Primary School, Leeds

All About Me

A rt is my favourite subject.
L earning is fun to do.
L ove my mummy and daddy.

A ctivities are fun for me.
B reak time I get to see all of my friends.
O ranges are my favourite fruit.
U nicorns are my favourite animal.
T eddies are my favourite to sleep with.

M arvellous Sri Lanka is my favourite country.
E choes are really fun for me.

Saheli Katugampola (6)
Cookridge Primary School, Leeds

All About Me

A pples are my middle favourite fruit.
L ike to do art and crafts.
L ike to go on play dates.

A mong Us is my favourite game.
B owling is the best.
O ranges are my middle favourite fruit.
U nicorns are my least favourite animal.
T eachers are the best.

M y favourite game is Roblox.
E lephants are my third favourite animal.

Joud Suleiman (6)
Cookridge Primary School, Leeds

All About Me

A mong Us is my favourite game.
L ove my mum so much.
L ove my cat so much.

A mazing swimming lessons.
B rilliant is my favourite beach ever.
O ptimus Prime is my favourite Transformer.
U p is my favourite movie.
T reasure is my second favourite game.

M ahdi is my best friend.
E nder Dragon is the final boss in my game.

Harry Lee (6)
Cookridge Primary School, Leeds

All About Me

A pples are my favourite fruit.
L ike Gorilla Tag a lot.
L ike my singing monsters.

A mong Us is weird.
B right mornings make me tired.
O riginally when I wake up my mom wakes me up.
U nusually I wake up early.
T ruthfully I wake up late.

M agical stuff is cool.
E verybody in my family is kind to me.

Nikita McMillan (7)
Cookridge Primary School, Leeds

All About Me

A wesome friend Zoe.
L ovely mummy I have.
L ovely brother I have.

A mazing daddy who helps.
B rilliant sausages Mummy cooks.
O utstanding friends are the best.
U nselfish Saheli, she is my friend.
T ruthful Zoe is the best.

M erry Santa gives us presents.
E xcellent Tabitha, I love her.

Emmeline (6)
Cookridge Primary School, Leeds

All About Me

A nimals with long tails are my favourite.
L earning new things is fun for me.
L ove my cat.

A gree with my friends.
B rightness hurts my eyes.
O pen-minded at school.
U nselfish person at school.
T rustworthy person.

M y English teacher is the best.
E nergetic is not my thing.

Rosalie Haworth (6)
Cookridge Primary School, Leeds

All About Me

A mazing at art and basketball.
L ove you Mummy and Daddy.
L ike to help my friend.

A pples are yummy.
B ubbles are fun.
O range is my favourite colour.
U s, in Class Three there's always a friend.
T alented at drawing.

M y mummy is funny and fun.
E xcellent at swimming.

Olivia Coetzee (7)
Cookridge Primary School, Leeds

All About Me

A mazing at football
L ove playing outside
L ike my house

A pples are my favourite fruit
B asketball I sometimes play
O ctober is my favourite month because of Halloween
U ltimate footballer
T alented at football

M agnificent at football
E nthusiastic about football.

Caleb Hughes-Powell (7)
Cookridge Primary School, Leeds

All About Me

A mazing at being a friend
L ove my mummy and daddy
L aughing with my friends

A nimals are my favourite thing
B rilliant at science
O utside is fun
U ltimate footballer
T alented at basketball and science

M y mummy and daddy are amazing
E xcellent scientist.

Charlie Halliday (6)
Cookridge Primary School, Leeds

All About Me

A pples are my favourite.
L earning is the best.
L ovely big school.

A utumn is my favourite season.
B rother, I love him.
O ctober is my second favourite season.
U nder my bed there is Lego.
T eddy is the best.

M y friend is Oliver.
E ating is the best.

Rory Burgener (6)
Cookridge Primary School, Leeds

All About Me

A mazing sports.
L ime with sugar is delicious.
L earning is fun.

A crisp is yummy but I like crisps.
B ubbly baths are nice.
O nions are yummy.
U nique spelling is fun.
T ea is yummy but it isn't my favourite.

M y name is Kyra.
E verything is fun.

Kyra Filipe (7)
Cookridge Primary School, Leeds

All About Me

A mong Us is my favourite game.
L ove my family.
L ove my games.

A t home, it is the best!
B eing alive is the best!
O utside is the best!
U sually, I wake up early.
T he school is fun.

M y friends are fun.
E veryone is fun.

George (6)
Cookridge Primary School, Leeds

All About Me

   A pples are the best.
   L ove my mummy.
   L ove my friends.

   A n artist when I grow up.
   B eing funny.
   O utside playing games.
   U pstairs I can play with my toys.
   T eddies are cute.

   M y friends and I play.
   E ating cake is the best.

Elaine Starkie (6)
Cookridge Primary School, Leeds

All About Me

A mazing at maths.
L ike science.
L ove phonics.

A pples are my favourite.
B rilliant at making stuff.
O ctober is my favourite.
U nder the ground, I dig.
T alented at tennis.

M agnificent pet.
E xcellent at swimming.

Jacob Cable-Watson (6)
Cookridge Primary School, Leeds

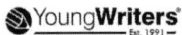

All About Me

A dog is my favourite animal.
L oving my friends.
L ike playing with my mummy.

A mazing work.
B aking with my nanny.
O utside is fun.
U nhappy days I can fix.
T rying my best.

M aking new friends.
E verything is fun.

Summer Lewis (6)
Cookridge Primary School, Leeds

All About Me

A wesome at Mario Kart
L ove my dogs
L ike tennis

A sk my mummy to play
B aths are my favourite
O utside having a sing
U ltimate swimmer
T alented at tennis

M agnificent teeth
E xcellent at singing.

Franklin Shirley (6)
Cookridge Primary School, Leeds

All About Me

A wesome at computing.
L ove maths.
L ove playing with Matey.

A mazing at running.
B rilliant at ideas.
O pen thoughts.
U ltimate friend.
T alented swimmer.

M agnificent hair.
E ndearing.

Oscar Fraser (6)
Cookridge Primary School, Leeds

Charlie P

A wesome at Lego and PE.
L ikes eating sweets.
L oves Nana.

A mazing at rolls and everything.
B rave.
O utstanding!
U nselfish.
T eam player.

M akes people laugh.
E njoys the hot tub.

Charlie Page (6)
Cookridge Primary School, Leeds

I Am Esther

A wesome at writing
L ikes eating doughnuts
L oves Olivia going to school.

A mazing at acrobatics
B rilliant
O utgoing
U nique
T alks a lot.

M akes people happy
E njoys dancing.

Esther Pierce (5)
Cookridge Primary School, Leeds

Emily

A wesome at art
L ikes eating strawberries
L oves Freya.

A mazing at discoing
B eautiful
O utstanding!
U pbeat
T eam player.

M akes people happy
E njoys being on holiday.

Emily McKirgan (5)
Cookridge Primary School, Leeds

Arin

A wesome at football
L ikes eating pizza
L oves Mum.

A mazing at basketball
B rilliant at reading
O utstanding
U pbeat
T eam player.

M akes people laugh
E njoys gaming.

Arin Konal (5)
Cookridge Primary School, Leeds

I Am Hudson

A wesome at football
L ikes eating pancakes.
L oves running.

A mazing at swimming
B rilliant
O utstanding
U nique
T alks a lot.

M akes people laugh
E njoys jumping.

Hudson Brookes (5)
Cookridge Primary School, Leeds

Martha

A wesome at painting.
L ikes eating crisps.
L oves hamsters.

A mazing at hugs.
B ouncy.
O utstanding!
U pbeat.
T eam player.

M akes people happy.
E njoys playing.

Martha Haigh (5)
Cookridge Primary School, Leeds

I Am Iris

A wesome at drawing
L ikes eating cakes
L oves animals.

A mazing at gymnastics
B eautiful
O utgoing
U nique
T remendous.

M akes people laugh
E njoys being alone.

Iris Pottage-Dixon (5)
Cookridge Primary School, Leeds

I Am Scarlett

A wesome at singing
L ikes eating ice cream
L oves jumping.

A mazing at drawing
B eautiful
O utgoing
U nique
T alks a lot.

M akes people giggle
E njoys dancing.

Scarlett Hufton-Alford (5)
Cookridge Primary School, Leeds

I Am Samuel

A wesome at football
L ikes eating chocolate
L oves Grandma.

A mazing at swimming
B rilliant
O utgoing
U nique
T remendous.

M akes people smile
E njoys school.

Samuel Wilkinson (5)
Cookridge Primary School, Leeds

I Am Jack

A wesome at football
L ikes eating orange
L oves Arlo.

A mazing at writing
B ashful
O utgoing
U nselfish
T alks a lot.

M akes people happy
E njoys Mummy.

Jack Gilder (5)
Cookridge Primary School, Leeds

I Am George

A wesome at Lego
L ikes eating carrots
L oves Mummy.

A mazing at building
B rave
O utgoing
U nselfish
T alks a lot.

M akes people smile
E njoys building.

George Haigh (5)
Cookridge Primary School, Leeds

Rawa

A wesome
L oveable
L ikes potato chips.

A mazing, I am good at football
B eautiful
O utstanding
U pbeat
T eam player.

M e, I am smart
E njoys football.

Rawa Aziz (5)
Cookridge Primary School, Leeds

George M

A wesome at Lego
L ikes eating cake
L oves Dad.

A mazing at writing
B rave
O utstanding
U pbeat
T eam player.

M akes people laugh
E njoys the hot tub.

George M (5)
Cookridge Primary School, Leeds

Seth

A wesome at football
L ikes eating pizza
L oves Dad.

A mazing at PE
B rave
O utstanding
U pbeat
T eam player.

M akes people laugh
E njoys playing.

Seth Dixon (5)
Cookridge Primary School, Leeds

Grace

A wesome at maths
L ikes eating crisps
L oves Mom.

A mazing at PE
B rave
O utstanding
U nselfish
T eam player.

M akes people happy
E njoys Barbie.

Grace Wardle (5)
Cookridge Primary School, Leeds

Dakota

A wesome at art
L ikes eating cake
L oves Mum.

A mazing at art
B eautiful
O utstanding!
U pbeat
T eam player.

M akes people laugh.
E njoys baking.

Dakota Wilson (6)
Cookridge Primary School, Leeds

I Am Sofia

A wesome at art
L ikes eating cake
L oves Olivia.

A mazing friend
B eautiful
O utgoing
U nique
T alks a lot.

M akes people happy
E njoys playing.

Sofia Kadiri (5)
Cookridge Primary School, Leeds

Dinosaur

D eadly and dangerous
I t lived a long time ago
N ice because they look like it to me
O mnivores, herbivores and carnivores
S uper cool and amazing
A mazing and can also eat other dinosaurs
U p in the air is a pterodactyl
R eally bad and furious.

Chaz Alain Villar (6)
Craigentinny Primary School, Edinburgh

T-Rex

D inosaurs are cool
I like T-rexes the most
N ow, they are extinct
O mnivores eat plants and meat
S tegosaurus
A live millions of years ago
U p in the sky, a pterodactyl
R oaming all over the land
S tomping around.

Archer Brown (7)
Craigentinny Primary School, Edinburgh

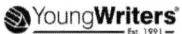

Gymnast

G ymnastics is my hobby
Y es, I am good at handstands
M y handstands are good
N ow, I know how to do a handstand
A handstand is my favourite
S plits are not my favourite
T oilet tig is my favourite, we play it in gymnastics.

Fajr (6)
Craigentinny Primary School, Edinburgh

Swimming

S plashing in the pool
W inning the swimming contest
I love swimming in the pool
M aking more friends
M aking splashes
I love to jump in the pool
N ow, I know how to swim
G oing to the first day of swimming.

Gabi (7)
Craigentinny Primary School, Edinburgh

Numbers

N ine is my favourite number
U sing a calculator
M aths is the best
B ig numbers up to 1,000,000,000
E ight is my second favourite number
R emembering times tables
S equencing numbers is fun.

Yousif Abdelmalik (7)
Craigentinny Primary School, Edinburgh

Gymnast

G ymnastics is my hobby
Y ou have to be flexible
M y gymnastics is good
N o one is as good as me
A gymnastic front flip
S o much fun
T wo backflips.

Lucia Salvador Neilson (6)
Craigentinny Primary School, Edinburgh

Drawing Is Fun

D rawing is fun
R ed is my favourite colour
A lways makes me happy
W ish I could draw all day
I love drawing
N ice pictures
G reat ideas.

Ella Oni (6)
Craigentinny Primary School, Edinburgh

Boxing

B oxing is my hobby
O n Monday, I want to do boxing
X -ray after my match
I went to boxing on Monday
N ext cap in boxing
G etting ready for boxing.

George Clayton (7)
Craigentinny Primary School, Edinburgh

Monkeys

M onkeys are my favourite animal
O nly ever climbing
N ice and soft
K ind
E veryone loves monkeys
Y es, super monkeys
S o cute.

Emily Wilson (7)
Craigentinny Primary School, Edinburgh

Drawing

D rawing is fun
R eally like colouring
A fun activity
W riting is good fun
I like to do it
N ow, I am writing this
G ood.

Louie Coleman (7)
Craigentinny Primary School, Edinburgh

Fraser

F unny and makes me laugh
R eally sporty
A dventurous boy
S uper at football
E veryone loves him
R eally cool.

Emma Gray (7)
Craigentinny Primary School, Edinburgh

Donuts Are Delicious

D elicious to eat
O ne is enough
N ice treat to have
U nder icing
T oppings are colourful
S weet and sticky.

Amirah Ali (7)
Craigentinny Primary School, Edinburgh

Happy

H opping makes me happy
A pples are healthy
P ow! My superpower is fun
P eople make me happy
Y ummy ice cream.

Gurjot Kaur (7)
Craigentinny Primary School, Edinburgh

Maths Is The Best

M aths is fun
A dding numbers together
T he best time is maths time
H undreds and thousands
S hapes are 2D and 3D.

Aisha Bayo (7)
Craigentinny Primary School, Edinburgh

Beach

B eautiful weather
E veryone having a nice day
A big sandcastle
C runchy seaweed
H ow beautiful it is.

Maahi (6)
Craigentinny Primary School, Edinburgh

Dogs

D ogs are snuggly and cute
O n their belly, they like a scratch
G o on walks
S uper eaters and they are sweet!

Mila Pele (6)
Craigentinny Primary School, Edinburgh

Froggy

F rogs are cool
R eally loud croaks
O n a lily pad
G reen and slimy
S wimming in a pond.

Theo Waterson (7)
Craigentinny Primary School, Edinburgh

Game

G oing to play Minecraft
A nd I like to play
M y favourite is Mario
E nd of play, Sonic.

Antos (7)
Craigentinny Primary School, Edinburgh

Kitties

C ats are so cute
A dorable cats
T ails that wiggle
S cratches scratching posts.

Mia Lawrie (6)
Craigentinny Primary School, Edinburgh

Adil

A bout me
D ay is fun
I like it in P3
L ots of bikes, I have two.

Adil Abedin (7)
Craigentinny Primary School, Edinburgh

Dogs

D ogs are cute
O ne has walks, Patch
G o for walks
S uper runners.

Reece Munro (7)
Craigentinny Primary School, Edinburgh

Cats

C ats are cute
A pink nose
T iny and friendly
S o fluffy.

Lily Hamilton (7)
Craigentinny Primary School, Edinburgh

Esmé Hunter

E verybody should be kind.
S ometimes go swimming with my dad.
M aybe change my fave colour.
É verybody gets to get played with.

H appy sometimes.
U nhappy when I cry.
N obody ever cries.
T oo cute to be a child.
E verybody should be happy.
R eally smart so I go to school.

Esmé Hunter (6)
Lambton Primary School, Lambton Village

Reeva Gallagher

R eally cool
E xcellent
E veryone is cool
V alentine's Day
A kind person.

G reen eyes
A mind reader
L ovely girl
L oves to help others
A lovely friend
G irly girl
H ide-and-seek
E xcellent
R osy cheeks.

Reeva Gallagher (6)
Lambton Primary School, Lambton Village

Amber Rose

A pples are nice.
M y friends are awesome.
B ananas are nice.
E very day I am good.
R osie is my bestie.

R oses are my favourite flower.
O ne of a kind.
S ometimes funny.
E veryone thinking happily.

Amber Malaugh (6)
Lambton Primary School, Lambton Village

Spider-Man

S uperpower
P eople love him
I ncredible Spider-Man
D on't go near the spider
E normous webs
R eally brave

M any crimes solved
A nother baddie to fight
N ever gives up.

Ethan Coult (7)
Lambton Primary School, Lambton Village

Isla Rees

I am *so* kind
S uper at doing stuff
L et everyone play with me
A great friend.

R eally nice
E veryone shares
E very day I take my dog on a walk
S haring with people.

Isla Rees (6)
Lambton Primary School, Lambton Village

Rosie-Ann

R eally cool.
O ranges are my favourite.
S trong I am.
I love my friend, Amber.
E verybody loves me.

A pples are good.
N obody has funnier games than me.
N ice Rosie-Ann.

Rosie-Ann Richardson (7)
Lambton Primary School, Lambton Village

Bowling

B asketball star.
O bstacles won't get in my way.
W ill listen to people, well, not strangers.
L oves bowling.
I love football too.
N ot bring up a fight.
G ets help and is brave.

Chukwukamso Onyeri (6)
Lambton Primary School, Lambton Village

Football

F ootball is my favourite
O pen pitch to run
O pposition won't get in
T otally awesome
B alls flying everywhere
A mazing goals
L ove football
L ots of cheering.

Connor Latimer (7)
Lambton Primary School, Lambton Village

Football

F ootball is the best.
O pen pitch on foot.
O ften play football.
T he football pitch.
B alls hit the net.
A ball is fun.
L oving every second.
L ots of cheering.

Dylan Kooner (6)
Lambton Primary School, Lambton Village

Football

F un at football
O nly out in the open outside
O nly sport for me
T eam spirit
B alls flying everywhere
A lways scoring goals
L ove football
L ots of cheering.

Rory Galer (6)
Lambton Primary School, Lambton Village

Harper

H appiness is important to me.
A nd I always come to school.
R uns around a lot.
P eople are kind to me.
E verything looks nice.
R eally kind.

Harper Steel (6)
Lambton Primary School, Lambton Village

Mam And Dad

M akes me happy.
A lways has a smile.
M akes me safe.

D oes make me laugh.
A lways is my dad.
D o love him so much.

Reenay Gallagher (6)
Lambton Primary School, Lambton Village

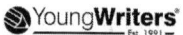

Roblox

R oblox is cool
O nly game for me
B uilding houses
L ove to play
O ne of the best games
X -ray mode is in Brookhaven.

Charlie Dawson (6)
Lambton Primary School, Lambton Village

Puppy

P erfect day today
U nderbelly rubs
P eople are cool
P lay with my puppies
"Y ippee!" my puppy said.

Saskia Espino-Byrne (6)
Lambton Primary School, Lambton Village

Peter

    P erfectly good
    E xtra cool
    T otally awesome
    E ats all the time
    R eally funny.

Peter Wilson (6)
Lambton Primary School, Lambton Village

Golf

G osh, I love golf
O nly sport for me
L ong range to go
F orth plays in the league.

Riley Latimer (7)
Lambton Primary School, Lambton Village

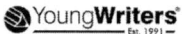

Things I Love

M inecraft is the best
E very day I like reading
L ove cute dogs
O ats are not the best
D rinking Sprite is the best
Y ellow is my favourite colour.

Melody Essienkan (6)
Seaton School, Aberdeen

About Georgia

G orgeous
E xcellent at gymnastics
O range is my favourite colour
R eally good at reading
G iggly
I ncludes everyone
A lways helping.

Georgia Singer (6)
Seaton School, Aberdeen

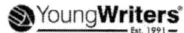

My Favourite Things

M inecraft is my game
O ms is my favourite YouTuber
S kittles are my favourite sweet
E njoy playing with my iPad
S paghetti is yummy.

Moses Souza (7)
Seaton School, Aberdeen

Things About Damon

D amon is funny
A nd Damon is good at football
M y favourite animal is a koala
O ctopuses, I don't like
N ow I am seven.

Damon Knox (7)
Seaton School, Aberdeen

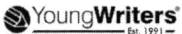

All About Me

A lways take care of our ocean
L ove cats
I am excellent at gymnastics
S uper at making friends
E njoy doing gymnastics.

Alise Kailovica (7)
Seaton School, Aberdeen

My Favourite Things

H orses are my favourite
A pples are the best
L emons are salty
I ce cream is the best sweet
N ever eat sweeties.

Halin Sattar (7)
Seaton School, Aberdeen

All About Willow

W illow is clever
I have a rabbit
L ong hair
L ong nails
O striches are funny
W inter is windy.

Willow Dow (7)
Seaton School, Aberdeen

My Favourite Things

A lot of science is what I like
X box is the best thing in the universe
E njoy Roblox on my computer
L ove my family.

Axel Olise (7)
Seaton School, Aberdeen

Stuff That I Like

R ed is my favourite colour
A pples are my favourite fruit
B eautiful
I like chocolate
A mazing at maths.

Rabia Al Masri (7)
Seaton School, Aberdeen

All About Me

N ice
A mazing
S uper at maths
I love kittens
F avourite colour is pink
A lways grateful.

Nasifa Akter (7)
Seaton School, Aberdeen

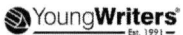

All About Me

N ela is pretty
E lephants are cute
L oving little bunnies
A nd apples.

Nela Melnicukova (6)
Seaton School, Aberdeen

All About Zach

Z is for Zach
A lways playing Xbox
C ats are fat
H ate my iPad.

Zach Dick (7)
Seaton School, Aberdeen

Beautiful

B irds in the sky, they glide and fly
E choes through the hills bring a tear to my eye
A s the sun shines down bright all day
U ntil the moon comes out to light the way
T his wonderful world, I have so much to see
I n Ireland my home for my family and me
F riends I have made in school are so cool
U mbrellas I have learned are such a good tool
L iving in Eskra is the best and St Patrick's School beats all the rest.

Ethan Power (6)
St Patrick's Primary School, Eskra

Environment

E nvironment is everything around us.
N ature walks with my family.
V olcanoes scare me!
I nsects are important to the environment.
R ain is important for growth.
O xygen, we need it to breathe.
N octurnal animals, bats and owls.
M y favourite thing in nature is a butterfly.
E co-Committee is in my school.
N ature Ranger Club in school.
T rees are part of nature.

Orlágh McRory (7)
St Patrick's Primary School, Eskra

Football Mad

F ootball is my favourite sport
O ut of all the rest
O utside playing is simply the best
T rying to practise all day
B est to get out early to play
A ll my friends love it too
L orcan and Senan to name a few
L ove it!

M ummy says I'm football mad
A nd it makes me glad
D efinitely, my biggest fan is Dad!

Páidí Shiels (6)
St Patrick's Primary School, Eskra

All About Me

S wimming is lots of fun
H appy I am with a bun
A nother thing I like to do
"Y ippee!" I say when I'm with my crew.

Q uick, quick, I can run
U nder, over, all done
I love to ride my bike
'N o' is not a word I like
N ow it's time for me to sleep tight.

Shay Quinn (6)
St Patrick's Primary School, Eskra

Football Is Fun

F un with my friends
O utside on the grass
O ver the bar
T op corner or a silly pass
B ounce, solo, score
A ll around the park
L ace up the boots
L et's all play football from morning until dark!

Football is fun!

Dara Gortland (6)
St Patrick's Primary School, Eskra

Football Fun

F ootball is so much fun.
O ver the bar, the ball goes.
O n the green grass, we play.
T eamwork is good.
B e awesome and
A lways pass the ball.
L ots of learning new skills.
L ots of fun in every game.

Conleth McGinley (6)
St Patrick's Primary School, Eskra

Outside

O utside is my favourite place to play
U mbrellas and wellies
T ricycles and bicycles
S andcastles and seashells
I cicles and snowballs
D aisy chains and berry picking
E verything I love about *outside!*

Maya McCaffrey (7)
St Patrick's Primary School, Eskra

Farming

F ields are where I keep my cows
A nimals in the shed
R olling in the grass having fun
M assey is the best
I love the farm
N ed helps to move the sheep
G reen grass for the silo pit.

Cillian Kelly (6)
St Patrick's Primary School, Eskra

Football

F ist passing.
O ver the bar.
O ur colours are black and white.
T ackle the ball.
B lock.
A ll my teammates together.
L earning new skills.
L ots of fun!

Oliver McAnespy (7)
St Patrick's Primary School, Eskra

Amy Rose

A pril Fools baby
M usic and dancing are the best
Y oung and fun.

R eally kind
O fficially beautiful
S ensitive and creative
E veryone's friend.

Amy Rose McGirr (6)
St Patrick's Primary School, Eskra

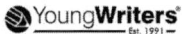

Let Me Say Hello

L orcan is my name
O thers like to call me Benj
R espect is nice to give
C ormac is my brother
A lso, I am a twin
N ew friends are always welcome.

Lorcan McGarvey (6)
St Patrick's Primary School, Eskra

Eskra

E veryone comes to play
S miling faces, hip, hip, hooray
K ick the ball, back of the net
R un and celebrate, we will win yet
A winning team - we are Eskra!

James McGirr (6)
St Patrick's Primary School, Eskra

Family

F orever friends
A lways together
M y best friends
I love my family
L ook out for each other
Y ou're special.

Conor McGinley (6)
St Patrick's Primary School, Eskra

My Cat

M alteser is her name.
Y es, I love my cat.

C ats are a good pet.
A mber loves her cat.
T oday I play with my cat.

Amber Lucas (6)
St Patrick's Primary School, Eskra

Nice To Meet You

S enan loves football
E very day I play with my friends
N ow I have started rugby
A lso, I am a twin
N ice to meet you.

Senan McGarvey (6)
St Patrick's Primary School, Eskra

Claire

C reative.
L oving.
A rtist.
I ncredible.
R elaxed.
E nergised.

Claire McMaugh (7)
St Patrick's Primary School, Eskra

Tallulah

T alking all the time
A pples
L ovely
L ove my friends
U nder the bar
L ove gymnastics
A spiring designer
H opeful.

Tallulah Tandy (5)
The John Wallis C of E Academy, Kingsnorth

Adelynn

A pple juice
D elicious cupcakes
E ggs scrambled
L ove playing
Y ummy unicorn cake
N early all gone
N ew toys for my birthday.

Adelynn Waters (6)
The John Wallis C of E Academy, Kingsnorth

Lilly-Rose

L ovely
I ce cream
L oving
L iving
Y ay!

R unner
O n top of the world
S pecial
E xcellent.

Lilly-Rose Harris (5)
The John Wallis C of E Academy, Kingsnorth

Lacey-Lou

L ovely
A mazing
C aring
E xcellent
Y ummy

L oving
O utstanding
U nderstanding.

Lacey-Lou Waller (5)
The John Wallis C of E Academy, Kingsnorth

Uwakmfon

U nderstanding
W arm
A mazing
K ind
M arvellous
F antastic
O utstanding
N ice.

Uwakmfon Monday (6)
The John Wallis C of E Academy, Kingsnorth

Yubaraj

Y ellow is the sun
U nder the
B lue shelter
A lways polite
R unning
A nd
J umping is fun.

Yubaraj Gurung (5)
The John Wallis C of E Academy, Kingsnorth

Olivia

O range
L ove my mum
I like rainbows
V ery good at running
I like smelling flowers
A mazing twin.

Olivia Omoniyi (5)
The John Wallis C of E Academy, Kingsnorth

Jackson

- **J** umping always
- **A** mazing
- **C** aterpillars I like
- **K** angaroo
- **S** mooth
- **O** ranges
- **N** early six.

Jackson Longstaff (5)
The John Wallis C of E Academy, Kingsnorth

Devian

- **D** elightful
- **E** ggs I like
- **V** ery kind
- **I** ncredible at maths
- **A** lways smiling
- **N** ever unhappy.

Devian Gurung (6)
The John Wallis C of E Academy, Kingsnorth

Octavia

O rangutan
C aring
T all
A mazing
V ery
I mportant
A chocolate ice cream.

Octavia Brown (5)
The John Wallis C of E Academy, Kingsnorth

Dana-Rose

D og
A pple
N ice
A mazing

R ed
O range
S illy
E ggs.

Dana-Rose Cooper (5)
The John Wallis C of E Academy, Kingsnorth

Archie

A pples
R eally cool
C hocolate ice cream
H appy
I like the colour blue
E xcited.

Archie Gibbs (5)
The John Wallis C of E Academy, Kingsnorth

Elaiya

- **E** xcellent reader
- **L** ove Mum
- **A** lways funny
- **I** ncredible
- **Y** ellow
- **A** spiring teacher.

Elaiya C (5)
The John Wallis C of E Academy, Kingsnorth

Aishna

A pples
I like eating pizza
S uper good at building
H opeful
N eat
A nd caring.

Aishna Pun Phagami (6)
The John Wallis C of E Academy, Kingsnorth

Ronnie

R abbit
O range
N early my birthday
N ext teacher
I mportant
E nergetic.

Ronnie Burgess (6)
The John Wallis C of E Academy, Kingsnorth

Bradley

B rilliant
R unner
A wesome
D igger
L ove
E xcellent
Y ap!

Bradley Rees (6)
The John Wallis C of E Academy, Kingsnorth

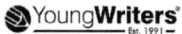

Hunter

H appy
U mbrellas
N ice
T alking
E ating apples
R eally like monkeys.

Hunter Harris (5)
The John Wallis C of E Academy, Kingsnorth

Ethan

E njoys buses
T rains at football
H as glasses
A mazing at football
N ice smile.

Ethan McDougall (5)
The John Wallis C of E Academy, Kingsnorth

Alyssia

A mazing
L ovely
Y ay!
S illy
S miley
I ce cream
A pples.

Alyssia Marsh (5)
The John Wallis C of E Academy, Kingsnorth

Rielle

R ed roses
I nsects
E xciting
L ovely
L ove my friends
E xcellent.

Rielle Watson (5)
The John Wallis C of E Academy, Kingsnorth

Olivia

O range lover
L ove
I ce cream
V ery kind
I nteresting
A mazing.

Olivia Suwala-Suwalski (6)
The John Wallis C of E Academy, Kingsnorth

Harley

H eart
A mazing
R eading a book
L ovely
E xcited
Y ou are cool.

Harley Stubbs (6)
The John Wallis C of E Academy, Kingsnorth

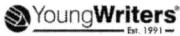

Jakub

J umping on trampolines
A pples
K ind to Caspar
U ntidy
B est at racing.

Jakub Jasinski (5)
The John Wallis C of E Academy, Kingsnorth

Garima

G irl
A pple
R ocket
I nsects
M cDonald's
A n ice cream.

Garima Gurung (5)
The John Wallis C of E Academy, Kingsnorth

Holly

H appy and helpful
O verly lovely
L ove my family
L ollipops
Y oghurts.

Holly Yarnell (5)
The John Wallis C of E Academy, Kingsnorth

Sophia

S mooth
O range
P olite
H appy
I like monkeys
A mazing.

Sophia Marchant (6)
The John Wallis C of E Academy, Kingsnorth

Pasang

P laying
A pples
S inging
A mazing
N ew shoes
G iggling.

Pasang Gurung (6)
The John Wallis C of E Academy, Kingsnorth

Thomas

T alkative
H appy
O kay
M agnificent
A wesome
S miley.

Thomas Butt (5)
The John Wallis C of E Academy, Kingsnorth

Lacey

L ove my teachers
A pples
C arrots
E nergetic
Y es, I am a twin.

Lacey Fuller (5)
The John Wallis C of E Academy, Kingsnorth

Mason

M aking friends
A pple juice
S leeping
O range
N ext policeman.

Mason Dray (6)
The John Wallis C of E Academy, Kingsnorth

Archer

- **A** pples
- **R** uns
- **C** ats
- **H** unter
- **E** ggs
- **R** eally funny.

Archer Harris (5)
The John Wallis C of E Academy, Kingsnorth

Lily

L ovely and cute
I am funny
L ove to paint
Y ellow like pineapples.

Lily Pietrzak (5)
The John Wallis C of E Academy, Kingsnorth

Denis

D inosaurs
E xtra chips
N ice
I ce cream
S ausages.

Denis Parker (5)
The John Wallis C of E Academy, Kingsnorth

Poppy

P retty
O ranges
P ink and purple
P izza
Y ummy.

Poppy Warren (6)
The John Wallis C of E Academy, Kingsnorth

Riha

R abbits
I like chips and juice
H appy
A lways playing.

Riha Ferdousi (6)
The John Wallis C of E Academy, Kingsnorth

Kase

K ind and caring
A mazing
S o good
E lephants.

Kase Williams (5)
The John Wallis C of E Academy, Kingsnorth

Ayla

A mazing
Y ummy yoghurt
L ovely
A dores hugs.

Ayla Karaoglan (5)
The John Wallis C of E Academy, Kingsnorth

Jay

J okes with Jakub
A lways laughing
Y ells at football.

Jay Gardiner (5)
The John Wallis C of E Academy, Kingsnorth

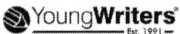

Dan

D ancing in my house
A pples and oranges
N ice.

Dan Paladi (5)
The John Wallis C of E Academy, Kingsnorth

Hope

H appy
O kay
P olite
E xcellent.

Hope Barrett (5)
The John Wallis C of E Academy, Kingsnorth

Leon

L ovely
E xcellent
O kay
N ice.

Leon Omoniyi (5)
The John Wallis C of E Academy, Kingsnorth

Noah

N ice
O ranges
A mazing
H appy.

Noah Pyke (5)
The John Wallis C of E Academy, Kingsnorth

Zak

Z oom very fast
A pples
K ick the ball.

Zakariya Khosravi (5)
The John Wallis C of E Academy, Kingsnorth

Young Writers Information

We hope you have enjoyed reading this book – and that you will continue to in the coming years.

If you're the parent or family member of an enthusiastic poet or story writer, do visit **www.youngwriters.co.uk/subscribe** and sign up to receive news, competitions, writing challenges and tips, activities and much, much more! There's lots to keep budding writers motivated!

If you would like to order further copies of this book, or any of our other titles, then please give us a call or order via your online account.

Young Writers
Remus House
Coltsfoot Drive
Peterborough
PE2 9BF
(01733) 890066
info@youngwriters.co.uk

Join in the conversation!
Tips, news, giveaways and much more!

YoungWritersUK   YoungWritersCW   youngwriterscw

Scan me to watch the This Is Me video!